TEEN LIFE™

FREQUENTLY ASKED QUESTIONS ABOUT

Growing Up as an Undocumented Immigrant

ROSEN
PUBLISHING®

New York

Lisa Wade
McCormick

I would like to thank four courageous DREAMers—Gaby Pacheco, Jose Ivan Arreola, Luz Ortiz, and Alain—for sharing their insights about the challenges they faced as undocumented immigrants growing up in this country.

Published in 2013 by The Rosen Publishing Group, Inc.
29 East 21st Street, New York, NY 10010

Library of Congress Cataloging-in-Publication Data

McCormick, Lisa Wade, 1961–
Frequently asked questions about growing up as an undocumented immigrant/Lisa Wade McCormick.—1st ed.
    p. cm.—(FAQ: Teen life)
Includes bibliographical references and index.
ISBN 978-1-4488-8329-5 (library binding)
1. Immigrant children—United States—Juvenile literature.
2. Children of illegal aliens—United States—Juvenile literature. I. Title.
JV6600.M33 2013
305.23086'9120973—dc23

                                                    2012018747

Manufactured in the United States of America

CPSIA Compliance Information: Batch #W13YA: For further information, contact Rosen Publishing, New York, New York, at 1-800-237-9932.

Contents

WHO ARE UNDOCUMENTED IMMIGRANTS?

Imagine growing up in a world where everything about your life had to be kept secret. You couldn't tell your classmates where you were born. You couldn't share any details about your family's background. And you lived in constant fear that your parents would be taken away and you'd never see them again.

This is the reality facing more than five million children in the United States. These are the children caught in the crossfire of the growing national debate over immigration.

At the heart of this controversy is how the United States should handle the immigrants who live in the country without legal documentation. These individuals are called undocumented immigrants. They are not U.S. citizens, although most hope they will be someday. Undocumented immigrants do not have the same rights as American citizens. For example, they can't legally vote or get a driver's license in this country.

Undocumented children are welcome at this safe house in Texas. But many of the country's approximately 5.5 million undocumented children are often treated with hatred because of their status.

According to the Pew Hispanic Center, there were approximately 11.2 million undocumented immigrants in the United States in 2010. Nearly half of those undocumented immigrants—about 46 percent—are the parents of young children. These adults have approximately 5.5 million children who are growing up in this country. America is the only home most of these children have ever known. But they say they're often treated like second-class citizens because of their status.

"This is a country of immigrants," said an undocumented immigrant who grew up in the Midwest. "But immigrants aren't always welcomed."

Changing Attitudes

A 2011 report published in the *Harvard Educational Review* confirms that Americans' attitudes about undocumented immigrants have changed in recent years. They've become harsher and less welcoming, according to the report *Growing Up in the Shadows: The Developmental Implications of Unauthorized Status.*

Undocumented immigrants often face hatred and discrimination. Some Americans say undocumented immigrants take jobs away from U.S. workers. Others say they don't pay taxes. There are also Americans who believe that undocumented immigrants shouldn't be allowed to stay in this country because they don't have the paperwork required to live here.

Those attitudes trickle down to schoolyards. "Little kids on playgrounds are being attacked or called nasty names because of their status," said Lisa Moore, gender and immigration project coordinator for the National Domestic Workers Alliance, in an interview with the author.

Undocumented children and their families are often labeled as "illegal aliens" or "illegals." "When people say the word 'illegal' [immigrant], it means 'criminal,'" said Gaby Pacheco, an undocumented immigrant who grew up in Miami, Florida, in an interview by phone. "In the eyes of a child, a criminal is a bad person. Words like 'alien' and 'illegal' are threatening."

Immigration experts, however, say it's not a criminal offense to be in the country without documentation. It's a civil issue, similar to getting a speeding ticket.

Many Americans, like these demonstrators in Ohio, favor tougher restrictions on undocumented immigrants. Several states have adopted strict immigration laws in recent years.

Tough New Immigration Laws

The negative attitudes toward undocumented immigrants are reflected in the flurry of laws recently passed in several states. In the first three months of 2011, lawmakers approved 1,538 immigration bills in twenty-six states, the report in the *Harvard Educational Review* said. Some of the laws give undocumented immigrants new opportunities, including letting them pay the lower in-state tuition at public universities. Most laws, however, impose harsh restrictions.

A second grader in Maryland airs concerns about the country's deportation of undocumented immigrants to First Lady Michelle Obama. America has deported a record number of undocumented immigrants in recent years.

In 2010, the state of Arizona enacted what the *New York Times* called "the nation's toughest bill on illegal immigration." The measure made the failure to carry immigration documents a crime. It also gave police the power to detain anyone they suspected was in the country illegally. The U.S. Supreme Court announced in December 2011 that it would review the law.

Other states have adopted similar "anti-immigrant" laws. Alabama, for example, passed a bill in 2010 that made it a crime to knowingly give a ride to an undocumented immigrant.

Children Caught in the Crossfire

Trapped in the middle of the angry rhetoric over the country's immigration policies are an estimated 5.5 million children, the Pew Hispanic Center said. One million of those children are undocumented. The remaining 4.5 million live in "mixed-status" households. In those homes, some children are U.S. citizens because they were born in this country. These "citizen children" have at least one parent who is undocumented. They may have siblings who are undocumented, too. These children's voices, however, are often ignored in the immigration debate.

"Largely absent from the discussion and nearly invisible in the portraits of the illegal immigrant population have been the millions of children living with unauthorized parents," a 2010 report by the Urban Institute said.

But these children consider themselves Americans in many ways. They attend the same schools as U.S. children. In 1982, the Supreme Court ruled that all children in this country—regardless of their immigration status—have a right to free public education from kindergarten through high school. This landmark decision came in the *Plyler v. Doe* case.

Undocumented students also enjoy the same movies and clothing as their U.S. classmates do. They like the same food and music. And they share the same dreams for their futures. According to the Immigration Policy Center, many of these "culturally American" children have little attachment to their homelands. But they're still undocumented immigrants, or they have immediate family members who are not authorized to be in this country. They can't escape that status or the difficulties it places on their lives. "These youth, who are American in spirit, schooling, and life experiences, are nonetheless illegal in the eyes of the law," the report in the *Harvard Educational Review* said.

Their "illegal" status often forces undocumented children and their families to live in the shadows of society. These families avoid many everyday tasks that U.S. citizens take for granted. Undocumented parents, for example, are often hesitant to call police if they're victims of a crime. Many are also hesitant to apply for food stamps or other services that their U.S.-born children need and can legally receive. "They don't want anyone to ask for their identification," Moore said.

These immigrants fear that if anyone discovers they're undocumented, the United States will force them to leave this country. That action is called deportation.

Undocumented immigrant Jose Ivan Arreola had nightmares as a child that his parents would be sent back to Mexico. "Having your parents deported was the scariest thing," said Arreola in a telephone interview. Arreola has lived in this country since he was four years old.

Why do millions of undocumented immigrants still decide to come to this country? Why do they leave their homelands? And what risks do they face on their journeys here?

Coming to America

"There are two types of undocumented people," Pacheco said. "There are those who came here on visas and then there are those who came across the border . . . Some kids remember the treacherous walk through Mexico and across the river."

Pacheco and her family came to the United States on visas, documents that allow immigrants to live and work in the country for a certain length of time. "My parents hired an attorney so we could stay here permanently," she said. The attorney, however, didn't file all the required paperwork. Pacheco and her family stayed after their visas expired. They became undocumented immigrants and were forced to live "under the radar."

A 2006 report by the Pew Hispanic Center revealed that 45 percent of undocumented immigrants came to the United States on visas and then stayed after those documents expired.

Undocumented immigrants cross rivers at night and brave other dangers to enter the United States. These immigrants are swimming across a river polluted with industrial waste and sewage to find a better life.

"Dangerous Odyssey"

The other 55 percent of undocumented immigrants entered the country without permission. Immigrants who cross the border illegally often face gangs, armed gunmen, and other dangers along their long journeys. Some immigrants pay "human smugglers"—called coyotes or snakeheads—thousands of dollars to sneak them or their families into this country.

A girl named Alejandra said smugglers brought her and her family across the border when she was thirteen years old. "It was pitch black when we ventured through the desert in Nogales into the U.S. territory," Alejandra wrote in a story for DreamActivists .org. "The smugglers were high on cocaine. They carried guns. They were lost and we had no choice but to follow…we were in their hands until my father paid our release."

Thousands of undocumented children also make the hazardous journey alone, without their families. These children risk their lives to find their parents, who left them in their homelands while they worked in the United States. Some families are separated for years.

In her book *Enrique's Journey*, author Sonia Nazario retraced the "dangerous odyssey" that a seventeen-year-old boy from Honduras took to find his mother in the United States. During her more than 1,600-mile (2,575 kilometers) journey, Nazario walked the same routes that Enrique took to America. She hopped the same buses that he rode across Central America. And she sat on top of the same freight trains that whisked Enrique through Mexico. Immigrant children who ride those trains call them *"El Tren de la Muerte"*—the Train of Death.

A Guatemalan teenager catches a ride on a northbound train to America to join his family. Each year, thousands of undocumented children ride "death trains" on their journeys to the United States.

"I lived with the near-constant danger of being beaten, robbed, or raped," Nazario wrote in her book. "Until my journey with migrant children, I had no true understanding of what people are willing to do to get here."

In Search of a Better Life

Many undocumented immigrants come to the United States to escape dangers in their homelands. Others come to America in hopes of a brighter future for their families. "My parents came here because they wanted better opportunities for me," said Arreola, the outreach manager for Educators for Fair Consideration (E4FC). The California organization helps undocumented students achieve their academic and professional goals. "There were no schools or jobs where I lived in Mexico."

Most undocumented immigrants in the United States—some 62 percent—are from Mexico, according to a 2010 report by the Office of Immigration Statistics. The next leading "source countries" are El Salvador, the Philippines, India, and China.

Records show the majority of undocumented immigrants live in California. The states with the next highest "undocumented" populations are Texas, Florida, and New York.

These undocumented immigrants face many challenges. Their children also face many difficulties growing up "undocumented" in this country. They can't, for example, get a job at their local supermarket. Their odds of going to college are slim. And they're always haunted with fears that authorities will take their parents away.

But they still have hope. They still dream of becoming U.S. citizens and getting good jobs. They're in America, after all. This is the land of opportunity. It's a country where anything is possible.

WHAT SETS UNDOCUMENTED YOUTHS APART?

On a cool December morning in 2011, dozens of children climbed the steps of the Cannon House Office Building in Washington, D.C. As the wind whipped across their faces, these young activists focused on the mission that had brought them to the nation's capital. They hoped the message they delivered to lawmakers that day would help millions of undocumented children and their families across the country.

Armed with more than five thousand handwritten letters, these children and immigration rights advocates walked through the Senate and House office buildings. They asked congressional leaders to consider their simple holiday wish: stop the deportations and detentions of undocumented immigrants that are "tearing families apart."

Fifteen-year-old Leslie Gonzalez of Georgia holds a sign in support of her mother, who she said was detained by U.S. authorities. Undocumented children constantly worry that the government will take their parents away.

The letters they delivered to lawmakers on both sides of the immigration debate echoed that same wish. "This year all I want is for my family to be together," a girl named Jacqueline wrote in her letter, which was featured on the Web site We Belong Together (http://www.webelongtogether.org). "I would really like your heart and patience to not deport my family, or as a matter of fact, any family."

An estimated 5.5 million children in the country share Jacqueline's dream. These are children who worry every day that their parents or other undocumented family members will be deported or locked up in facilities called detention centers.

In his letter, a boy name Dennis said he was scared that immigration officials would deport his father. "If they deport him, we would have to go to Matamoros, Tamaulipas...where there is more and more violence every day."

Growing Up in Fear

As an undocumented girl growing up in the Midwest, Luz Ortiz was always afraid that her family would be sent back to Mexico. She didn't share this fear with her classmates. She kept it secret. She couldn't risk anyone finding out about her family's background. Ortiz came to the United States with her mother and two siblings when she was eleven years old. They joined her father, who had worked here for five years.

"I imagined situations where we'd all get deported," Ortiz said in a telephone interview. "It was always a fear of mine that we'd get deported or my parents would get caught in a raid [at their jobs]."

Immigration agents often check restaurants, meatpacking plants, and other businesses to find unauthorized workers. These are called work-site raids.

An undocumented immigrant named Alain, who spoke with the author, also grew up with fears that his parents would be deported. Those worries are still etched in his memory. "I'm the oldest out of three kids and I worried how I, as a twelve- or thirteen-year-old, would be able to take care of my younger brother and sister if my parents were taken away," said Alain, who was afraid to use his last name because of his immigration status.

Undocumented immigrant Francisca Lino, mother of six, publicly asked U.S. authorities to delay her deportation. Immigration rights activists say families are "shattered" when undocumented parents are deported or detained.

Those fears turned into reality for a nine-year-old girl named Daisy. She came home from school and discovered that immigration agents had taken her parents away. "They were sent back to Mexico," Daisy wrote on the We Belong Together Web site. "Now my sister [thirteen] takes care of me, but I miss my parents. When am I going to see them again?"

"Shattered Families"

Thousands of children with undocumented parents have asked that same question. These are the children who get left behind when their parents are deported or sent to a detention center. And their numbers are growing.

The United States deported a record number of undocumented immigrant parents in recent years. Many of their children are U.S. citizens because they were born here. Their status, however, doesn't protect their parents from these enforcement actions. Between 1998 and 2007, the United States deported more than 108,000 undocumented parents, a report by the Department of Homeland Security showed.

The crackdown continues. In the first six months of 2011, the United States forcibly sent more than forty-six thousand undocumented parents back to their homelands, according to a report by the Applied Research Center (ARC). "This means that almost one in four people deported is the parent of a United States citizen child," lead researcher Seth Freed Wessler told the Huffington Post. Wessler wrote ARC's report *Shattered Families,* which warned: "These deportations shatter families and endanger the children left behind."

Children with undocumented parents also suffer when their mothers and fathers are sent to one of the 350 detention centers across the country. The United States placed 363,000 unauthorized immigrants in detention centers in 2010, according to ARC's report. Immigrants are held for days, weeks, or months while the government decides if they can stay in the country.

Foster Care Nightmares

What happens to the children when their parents are detained or deported? Some stay with family members. But a growing number are forced to live with strangers—in foster care.

"Thousands of children enter the child welfare system and are often stuck there," Wessler told the Huffington Post.

According to ARC's report, at least 5,100 children were placed in foster care in 2010 after their parents were sent to detention centers or deported. Some of those children may never see their parents again. "The children face enormous obstacles to rejoining their parents," the Huffington Post said.

Josefina and Clara's Story

Undocumented sisters Josefina and Clara have tried for more than a year to find their children, who they say are "lost" in the foster care system.

According to the *Shattered Families* report, the women's nightmare started in 2010 when U.S. Immigration and Customs Enforcement (ICE) agents searched their home for drugs. Agents didn't find any narcotics, but they took the undocumented sisters into custody. Their children—a nine-month-old, a one-year-old, and a six-year-old—were placed with child protective services.

The sisters stayed in a detention center for four months. In December 2010, authorities deported them to Mexico. Their children stayed behind. A year later, these families are still torn apart. "I have no contact with my baby," Josefina said in ARC's report. "I didn't do anything wrong to have my children taken from me."

Emotional Scars

Undocumented immigrant Gaby Pacheco works with families who have loved ones in detention centers. She's seen the emotional

Arizona authorities arrest a man during a 2009 work-site raid. Undocumented immigrants caught in these raids are often detained or deported. They're separated from their families for months or years.

scars left on children by these actions. "These are kids who were in loving homes and they are not able to understand why their parents are there [in detention centers]," she said. "It wasn't like these were kids who were abused or in a bad situation."

Pacheco has also seen the devastating effects deportations have on children. "When parents get deported, it's a huge struggle for them to reunite with their families," she said. "Many times it takes two to three years. And if there's no family around, these children get lost in the foster care system."

Immigration rights groups say children suffer in many ways when they're separated from their parents because of these enforcement actions. "When this happens, children can face poverty because their parents aren't there to pay the bills anymore," the We Belong Together Web site states. "Older children can be forced to take on new responsibilities, like taking care of younger siblings, and this can make them tired and worried." These children can also have trouble in school or health problems.

Emergency Plans

Some undocumented parents make emergency plans to protect their children in case they are detained or deported. The plans describe who will take care of their children while they are gone.

A 2010 survey revealed 58 percent of undocumented Latino parents polled had emergency plans for their children. The survey also found that 40 percent of those parents had discussed the plans with their children, according to the *Growing Up in the Shadows* report in the *Harvard Educational Review*.

Other undocumented parents, however, don't talk to their children about these issues. They wait until their children are in their early teens to discuss their immigration status. These parents hope they can protect their children from the harsh realities associated with their status, the report said. Their decisions, however, only postpone "difficult and alienating" conversations.

Early Lessons in Differences

Undocumented immigrant Luz Ortiz knew her status when she was in elementary school in the Midwest. She also understood the limitations it placed on her life. "Even getting into school was a challenge," said Ortiz. "You needed a Social Security number for the whole process." Her school, however, made an exception and let her in. "I was the first undocumented immigrant," she said.

Ortiz and other undocumented immigrants also knew they were different than their American classmates. Many had different colored skin. They spoke with accents. Some couldn't speak or read English. "It was in third or fourth grade that I began to understand what it meant to be different," said undocumented immigrant Jose Ivan Arreola. "The differences came in racial terms. The kids told me I was 'brown' and I looked different."

Arreola also sounded different when he spoke. "The kids made fun of me because of my accent," he said. He now speaks perfect English with little hint of an accent.

Ortiz had a similar experience. "I was in an English school, and I didn't speak English," she said. "I was also not middle class, and my classmates had more money. And the fashions were different than where I came from in Mexico."

Not a Normal Childhood

By the time these and other undocumented students reach middle school, the differences between them and their U.S.

classmates become even clearer. Most of their parents, for example, work multiple jobs for low wages. Their families often live in poverty. And they rarely get a chance to have a "normal" childhood like most American kids.

"It's hard to have a stereotypical childhood when you're undocumented and poor," Arreola said. "In my free time, I had to help my father or my uncles with landscaping, roofing, or construction."

Undocumented students face even more challenges in high school. They discover issues that set them even farther apart from their U.S. classmates. Those issues also threaten their hopes for the future and their chances to achieve the American dream.

Myths and Facts

 Undocumented children who grow up in this country do not want to become U.S. citizens.

Fact: ➡ Most undocumented children want to become U.S. citizens. But there is no easy path to achieve that goal. It is a long and complicated process that can take years. It is not as simple as filling out a form and paying a fee. The *Growing Up in the Shadows* report in the *Harvard Educational Review* said the road to citizenship for undocumented immigrants is blocked. "Today, there is no avenue to provide a pathway to citizenship for the unauthorized," the report said.

 Undocumented children and their families do not pay taxes.

Fact: ➡ Undocumented immigrants pay billions of dollars in taxes each year, according to the Immigration Policy Center. They pay sales taxes and property taxes. At least half pay income taxes. The Institute for Taxation and Economic Policy (ITEP) said unauthorized immigrants paid $11.2 billion in state and local taxes in 2010. That included $1.2 billion in personal income taxes, $1.6 billion in property taxes, and $8.4 billion in sales taxes.

Undocumented children and their families drain social service agencies in the United States.

Fact: ➡ Undocumented children and their families are not legally eligible for any social services that require documentation. Some undocumented immigrant families receive aid for their U.S.-born "citizen children." Others are afraid to ask for assistance because they don't want anyone to discover their status. A 2006 study by the Texas comptroller also revealed that undocumented immigrants paid approximately $424.7 million more in state taxes than they used in such services as education and health care. That reflected a net benefit to the state.

HOW DO UNDOCUMENTED TEENS FIT IN?

Tragedy struck a small Texas community near the Mexican border in late 2011. A promising teenager—known for his smile and playing the electric guitar—kissed his mother goodnight and changed into his favorite maroon shirt and striped black tie. He then walked into his family's bathroom and took his own life.

Family members said the high school senior had given up hope that he'd get into college. He no longer believed that he could achieve his dream of becoming an engineer. But eighteen-year-old Joaquin Luna was a bright student. He was in the top 20 percent of his class at Benito Juarez-Abraham Lincoln High School in Mission, Texas. The school's principal said he was "bound for greatness," according to a story in the *Monitor*, a Texas newspaper.

Diyer Mendoza has many pictures of his brother, Joaquin Luna, in his home. Eighteen-year-old Luna committed suicide because he was undocumented and feared he'd never go to college, Mendoza says.

Luna, however, was an undocumented student. He'd lived in the United States since he was six months old, but he didn't have the paperwork required to be a citizen.

The Hidalgo County sheriff's office ruled Luna's death a suicide. But investigators didn't have a motive. Luna's family did. "I know he did it because of his legal status," his half-brother Diyer Mendoza told the *Los Angeles Times*.

Luna understood the limits his status placed on his future, Mendoza said. He knew that many colleges and universities wouldn't accept him because he was undocumented. "When he would submit the application, he would tell us the first thing that pops up was: 'Are you a citizen?' 'Are you a legal resident?' or 'Do you have a Social Security number?" Mendoza told the *Monitor*. "And he didn't, and so from there he would get shut down."

Immigration right activists in Texas called Luna's death "a symbol of the psychological toll" that is taken on undocumented youth in this country, according to a story in the *New York Times*.

"Their Worlds Turn Completely Upside Down"

High school is an especially difficult time for undocumented students, according to researchers who've studied these young immigrants. "In late adolescence, they start to realize their legal limitations, and their worlds turn completely upside down," sociologist Roberto G. Gonzales told the *New York Times*.

During their high school years, undocumented students discover they can't experience the same rites of passage as their U.S. classmates. These students, for example, can't get a driver's license because they don't have a Social Security number. They can't legally get a job or vote either. Adding to those missed opportunities is the constant fear that they or a loved one will be deported. "Because of their immigration status, their day-to-day lives are severely restricted and their futures are uncertain," Gonzales wrote in a report for the Immigration Policy Center.

Going to college is also difficult for the estimated sixty-five thousand undocumented students who graduate from U.S. high schools each year. Grades aren't blocking their entrance, though. "They are honor roll students, athletes, class presidents, valedictorians, and aspiring teachers, engineers, and doctors," Gonzales wrote.

During her senior year in high school, undocumented immigrant Luz Ortiz discovered that her college dreams might disappear. "I learned there were a whole bunch of colleges I couldn't attend," said Ortiz, who was the valedictorian of her class. Ortiz was missing one piece of information that colleges request on their applications—a nine-digit Social Security number. Her American dream started to fade. "After hearing 'no, no, no,' it was depressing," Ortiz said. "School has always been one of my passions."

Missed Rites of Passage

Undocumented teens miss other rites of passage during their high school years. One of the biggest is getting a driver's license. "I had a certificate saying I had completed the hours [of driver's education] and was ready to get my license," Pacheco said. "But when I went to the Department of Motor Vehicles, they said I couldn't get my license because of my status."

Finding a job is also difficult for undocumented teens. Alain, for example, knew he couldn't work at the same places as his American classmates. "I couldn't go to a place like Best Buy and ask for a job because of my status," he said. "It made me feel bad, but I knew what stores would want [a Social Security number], and I knew I didn't have one."

Alain's father owned a small business. "I would go and help him in the summer," he said. "And if my friends asked me where I was working, I'd say, 'At my dad's shop.'"

Undocumented immigrant Jose Ivan Arreola didn't share many high school milestones with his classmates either. "I remember not being able to drive, vote for the first time, or get a job," he said.

Hate Speech and Ignorance

Arreola experienced some painful moments during high school. "The most challenging days to be at school were the ones when immigration came up in class," he said. "I had to listen to a lot of hate speech and ignorance."

An undocumented student named Ingrid also heard hateful comments from a wealthy businessman in her community. During her senior year in high school, Ingrid's vice principal invited her to a formal dinner with local leaders. "There were two things of which she asked me not to speak: politics and my immigration status," Ingrid wrote in a story for the Educators for Fair Consideration advocacy group.

Ingrid followed that advice. Throughout the evening, she talked to an older businessman about everything from finance to his expensive cars. "We conversed...as if he and I were no different," she wrote. "I was beginning to feel comfortable."

Her comfort turned to despair when the man asked about her school's policy regarding undocumented students. Ingrid's teacher said the school didn't have one. The man then turned to Ingrid. "I do not want to sponsor aliens who will take away opportunities that students like you deserve," he told her. The words pierced Ingrid's heart. "The heavy sensation in my chest did not go away," she wrote.

"No Chess Club or Drama Society for the Kids"

In 2011, lawmakers in Alabama passed a bill that took away many rites of passage from undocumented students in kindergarten through twelfth grade. The Alabama Taxpayer and Citizen Protection Act prohibited undocumented immigrants from "participation in any extracurricular activity outside of the basic course of study."

"In other words, no chess club or drama society for the kids," Tim Murphy wrote in a story for the *Mother Jones* Web site (http://motherjones.com). "Football might be a religion in Alabama, but that's off-limits too." The story's headline read: "Alabama to Undocumented Kids: No Prom For You!"

High Rates of Depression

These missed rites of passage and negative attitudes toward undocumented immigrants take an emotional toll on the young students' lives.

"Typically, the sources of stress for most people are money, school, work, relationships, and health," author and professor William Perez said in a story on the DRM Capitol Group's Web site (http://drmcapitolgroup.com). The organization calls itself a "voice" for undocumented youth in our nation's capital. "Undocumented students have the same sources of stress that everybody has," Perez said, "but their immigration status adds to that amount of stress they face every day."

Undocumented college students hold hands in December 2010 as the U.S. Senate votes on a bill that would open the doors of citizenship for them. The DREAM Act failed to advance.

Undocumented students say they often feel unwanted or isolated. They move toward a state of "perpetual outsider-hood," according to a report in the *Harvard Educational Review*.

Some also suffer serious mental health issues. "There are really high rates of depression by these [undocumented] youth," said Lisa Moore of the National Domestic Workers Alliance. "They've been told by their parents to study hard and make something of themselves. But in high school, these kids start to think 'Why should I care' if I'm not going to be able to go to college and get a job?"

Undocumented teen Octavio Rojas loads a box of blackberries at a Georgia farm. Some undocumented teenagers are forced to drop out of high school and help support their families.

Moore worked extensively with undocumented students in the 1990s for an organization in California. "I've seen great students drop out of school after they discovered their efforts may not come to anything," she said, adding that thoughts of suicide are not uncommon among these teens. "They hear it's a waste of money to go to college because they won't be able to work in their fields."

Little Time to Be a Teenager

Financial pressures at home also force some undocumented students to drop out of high school. They're students like nineteen-year-old Brenda, who crossed the U.S.-Mexico border when she was seven years old.

"I had to leave high school a month before graduation because my family needed help paying the bills," Brenda wrote in a story for Minnesota National Public Radio. "I help take care of the little kids, and I work a second shift in a factory. I don't have a lot of time to be a teenager or to have fun." Immigration agents raided the company where Brenda's mother worked. "She didn't have the right papers, so she lost a job she'd had for twelve years," Brenda wrote. "That had a big effect on our lives."

The teen immigrant, however, still dreams of graduating from high school and attending college. "I hope someday there'll be a better life open to me in the United States," she wrote. "I want things to change for families like mine."

Remember Joaquin Luna? He came closer than he knew to reaching his dream. The University of Texas–Pan American accepted his application, according to a story by Manny Fernandez in the *New York Times*. Luna, however, never found out. He died before his admission was approved.

chapter four

HOW CAN UNDOCUMENTED TEENS ACHIEVE THEIR DREAMS?

A high school senior and her teacher exchanged "heated" words in Spanish one February morning in 2011. The San Francisco teenager had learned that Harvard University—the prestigious Ivy League school founded in 1636—wanted to interview her as a potential student. But Lourdes didn't want to meet with recruiters from the oldest university in the country.

She had her reasons. They're ones shared by millions of children across the United States. The promising California student was an undocumented immigrant. She lived in constant fear of deportation.

Her teacher, however, hoped that fear wouldn't stop Lourdes from chasing her college dreams. "Harvard and Stanford are the only two places I know of where undocumented students [can] get a full ride," teacher Amadis Velez told *Mother Jones*.

Odds Stacked Against Undocumented Students

But the odds of Lourdes—or any undocumented student—attending college in the United States are slim. Less than 20 percent of the undocumented students who graduate from U.S. high schools pursue a college degree, according to research organizations such as the Pew Hispanic Center and the Urban Institute.

"It's remarkable for undocumented students to even apply to college," an immigrant named Irving said in the film *American Dream Seekers*. The advocacy group Educators for Fair Consideration made the movie.

Undocumented immigrant Gaby Pacheco said her high school counselor discouraged her from applying to college. The counselor shared that advice after she learned Pacheco's immigration status. "She was afraid for me and my family," the honor student said. "She was worried that if I applied to college, I might get myself and my family in trouble and we could get deported."

Bans Against College-Bound Undocumented Students

Some states have taken action making it more difficult for undocumented immigrants to go to college. Two states passed legislation that ban undocumented students from enrolling in public colleges and universities. South Carolina became the first in 2008 when lawmakers approved the Illegal Immigration Reform Act,

Nelly Rodriguez of Kansas joins a mock graduation in Washington, D.C., to show support for the DREAM Act. The bill, which had not passed by mid-2012, would open more college doors for undocumented students.

according to the National Conference of State Legislatures (NCSL). Alabama approved a similar law in June 2011.

Some public colleges and universities have also adopted policies that make it nearly impossible for undocumented immigrants to attend the schools. In Virginia, for example, many four-year state schools require students to show proof of citizenship or legal residency, according to the nonprofit College Board. "And [the schools] refuse admission to students without documentation. This policy is not, however, a state law."

Biggest Obstacle: Money

Undocumented students who dream of attending college face an even bigger obstacle. It's money—or the lack of money and other financial resources.

Nearly 40 percent of undocumented students live below the poverty line, according to the E4FC. Students in those households are often forced to find jobs and help support their families. There is little money left for college. And financial aid to help cover the spiraling costs of higher education isn't an option for these students. "Based on current government policies, undocumented students cannot qualify for federal or state-based financial aid, including grants, work-study jobs, or loan programs," a report by E4FC stated.

Full-time students pay $15,000 to $40,000 a year to go to college, the organization said. "Without financial aid, the costs of attending a college can often be prohibitive for undocumented students and their families."

Undocumented immigrant Tania Chavez understands those financial struggles. The aspiring accountant said paying for college has taken a costly toll on her family. "Paying rent, bills, and school is too much for my mother," Chavez told KCET public television. "We try to save; we buy only the food we need; we try to not eat out; I usually borrow my books from friends instead of buy them."

Chavez once used the tips her mom made as a waitress to pay for tuition. "I had to pay in all singles [bills]," she said during the KCET interview.

In-State vs. Out-of-State Tuition

In many states, public colleges and universities require undocumented students to pay the more expensive out-of-state tuition. Twelve states, however, offered in-state tuition breaks to undocumented students at the end of 2011, according to the NCSL. Those states were California, Connecticut, Illinois, Kansas, Maryland (community colleges), Nebraska, New Mexico, New York, Rhode Island, Texas, Utah, and Washington. Wisconsin passed a similar law in 2009 but revoked the measure in 2011.

To receive those in-state discounts, undocumented students had to meet specific requirements. They had to live in the state, attend a high school in the state for at least one year, and graduate or receive a General Educational Development (GED) certificate in the state.

Some public colleges and universities in Minnesota also offer in-state tuition breaks to all students, including undocumented immigrants.

Marisol Conde-Hernandez speaks in support of laws that would let undocumented students pay lower, in-state college tuition in New Jersey. The undocumented teen holds up an academic achievement award that she won in high school.

Four states, however, have passed laws that ban undocumented students from paying the cheaper in-state tuition. Those states are Arizona, Colorado, Georgia, and Indiana.

Private Colleges and Universities

The doors to private colleges and universities are usually more open to undocumented students than public schools, researchers said. Most private schools consider undocumented immigrants "international students." Undocumented students must then compete with students from all over the world for a "handful of enrollment slots," the E4FC report said.

Money is still a major roadblock. Private colleges can cost $80,000 to $200,000 for four-year degrees. Many of those schools also look at a student's ability to pay the entire four years. That's worrisome news to undocumented students with limited financial resources. "Because of these policies, thousands of qualified and competitive undocumented students are denied admission to private colleges every year," the E4FC report said.

Community colleges, which offer associate's degrees, are another option for undocumented students, researchers said. They're less expensive than four-year schools and are generally more willing to accept students without documentation.

Private Funding Scarce

To reduce the soaring costs of higher education, undocumented students can apply for private scholarships. But they have little chance of getting money from those sources. "Undocumented students are not eligible for most private scholarships, which typically require U.S. citizenship or permanent legal residence," the E4FC report said.

Some undocumented students question the logic behind those scholarship rules. "If we get just a little help, then I think we'll become some of the strongest students and most successful people," said undocumented student Irving in *American Dream Seekers.*

Beating the Higher-Education Odds

Thousands of undocumented students have already beaten the odds stacked against them and achieved their college dreams. According to the E4FC, undocumented college-bound students share similar traits:

- They've lived in the United States for most of their lives.

- Their parents brought them to the country at a young age.
- They can speak English.
- They consider themselves Americans.
- They attended elementary, middle, and high school in the United States.
- They excelled academically in high school.
- They don't have a way to become a legal resident or U.S. citizen.

Those characteristics describe undocumented students like Luz Ortiz. This honor student originally wanted to study engineering at Kansas State University in Manhattan, Kansas. But she couldn't afford the school's out-of-state tuition. Ortiz, however, didn't abandon her college dream. She found a private university in Kansas City, Missouri, that accepted undocumented students and fit her limited budget. In May 2012, Ortiz graduated with a degree in graphic arts from Avila University.

Undocumented immigrant Gaby Pacheco is another successful college graduate. She went to Miami Dade College and has three degrees in education.

Undocumented immigrant Jose Ivan Arreola credits his parents and teachers for much of his academic success. "I was fortunate that I never had a teacher, counselor, or adult tell me that going to college was not a possibility," he said. "I had a lot of teachers who encouraged me and invested in me and my education. My parents guided me through college and served as a source of inspiration."

Undocumented student Noheli Carrasco is active in her Virginia high school's Junior ROTC program. Carrasco wants to join the air force but can't unless lawmakers pass the DREAM Act.

Finding money for college was a challenge, though. Arreola said his high school English teacher helped him navigate those choppy financial waters. "He put in an enormous amount of research and found Santa Clara University [a Jesuit school in California]," Arreola said. "He also empowered me to do my own research and helped me find a way to make college a reality."

Arreola's hard work paid off. "I was very blessed to get a college education for free," he said. "I got full scholarships."

Challenges Ahead

After he graduated, Arreola landed a job as an outreach manager for E4FC. Other undocumented college graduates aren't as lucky. In 2011, undocumented immigrant Alain earned a bachelor's degree in finance from a private Midwestern university. He wants to work in the banking industry. But he can't get a job because of his status and lack of documentation.

Some undocumented students start work on their college degrees but never get the chance to finish. They're students like twenty-four-year-old Viridiana Martinez of North Carolina. Her college dream ended in 2011 because she couldn't produce a valid visa, according to a story on National Public Radio (NPR). The former honor student is now a full-time activist for immigration rights. She's part of a growing movement among undocumented students who are talking publicly about their status and the limitations it places on their dreams.

These young activists hope their actions will convince lawmakers to pass legislation that would open the door of citizenship to millions of undocumented immigrants. They know they're facing an uphill battle. But they're ready to fight—for themselves and other undocumented students who hope to achieve their American dreams.

Ten Great Questions to Ask a Counselor

1 Whom can I trust?

2 What is my immigration status?

3 What are the laws in my state about undocumented immigrants?

4 How can I find out about resources available to undocumented immigrants and their families in my community?

5 Where can I get information about summer jobs?

6 Can I play sports or participate in other school or extracurricular activities?

7 What should I do if my parents are deported?

Where can I get help for depression?

Where can I find information about college?

Where can I get information about financial aid and scholarships available to undocumented students?

WHAT DOES THE FUTURE HOLD FOR UNDOCUMENTED STUDENTS?

On a cool Friday morning in January 2010, undocumented immigrant Felipe Matos stood on the steps of the historic Freedom Tower in downtown Miami, Florida. The twenty-three-year-old honor student at St. Thomas University was about to take his first step on what immigration rights supporters now call the Trail of Dreams. Matos and three other student activists—Gaby Pacheco, Carlos Roa, and Juan Rodriguez—organized the 1,500-mile (2,414 km) march from Miami to Washington, D.C., to air their concerns about the daunting challenges that millions of undocumented immigrants in this country face.

These young protesters were brought to the United States as children by their parents. They'd grown up in an America that some undocumented immigrants call the "golden cage"—a place where they could live and work but never have true freedom. "They have spent their

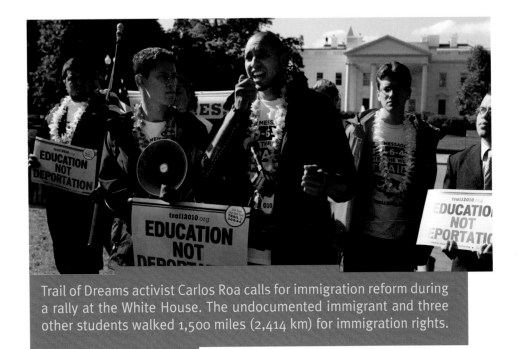

Trail of Dreams activist Carlos Roa calls for immigration reform during a rally at the White House. The undocumented immigrant and three other students walked 1,500 miles (2,414 km) for immigration rights.

childhoods in fear and hiding, unable to achieve their real potential," according to a press release posted on trail2010.org.

Matos, for example, wants to become a teacher, according to a story in the *New York Times*. But the young scholar may never get the chance because he doesn't have a valid Social Security number. His fellow "dream" walkers worry about their futures, too. Pacheco wants to become a music therapist and work with autistic children. Roa hopes to become an architect. And Rodriguez wants to be a sociologist.

"Our Present Is Unbearable"

These promising students took their dreams and frustrations to the streets—and ultimately to the White House—during their four-month march to the nation's capital. They knew their journey was dangerous. As undocumented immigrants, three of the walkers—Matos, Pacheco, and Roa—faced possible deportation with every step. Rodriguez, a native of Colombia, became a legal resident in 2008. "We are aware of the risk," Matos said in an interview with the *New York Times*. "We are risking our future because our present is unbearable."

Throughout their trek, the students met with local residents, elected officials, and groups that supported and opposed immigration reform. They shared their visions of a country where undocumented students who came to the United States as children could go to college, get jobs, and become citizens. "Everybody understands what it feels like to have a dream," Matos told the *Falcon Times*, the student newspaper for Miami Dade College.

Many people rallied around the students and their cause. Others spewed hatred at them. Just outside a small town in Georgia, members of the Ku Klux Klan called the students "Mexican dogs," *ABC News* reported. In North Carolina a man looked at Matos and said, "You're not completely human," a story on ARC's Web site, Colorlines.com, said.

The words stung. But the students ignored the ugly remarks. "Pacheco and her friends…said slander would not distract them from their goal: immigration reform that might bring them U.S. citizenship," the *ABC News* report said.

The DREAM Act

A bill introduced on Capitol Hill in 2001 could help undocumented youth achieve that goal. The measure is called the Development,

Relief, and Education for Alien Minors Act—or DREAM Act, for short. The bill is designed to open a door to citizenship for undocumented students who meet specific requirements. President Barack Obama's White House Web site states, "It's limited, targeted legislation that will allow only the best and brightest young people to earn their legal status after a rigorous and lengthy process."

The Dream Act applies to undocumented immigrants who:

- Entered the country as children at age fifteen or younger
- Have lived continuously in the country for five years
- Have good moral character
- Pass a criminal background check
- Have graduated from a U.S. high school, obtained a GED, or been accepted to a college or university in this country
- Are thirty-five or younger when the act becomes law

According to the proposed law, undocumented immigrants who meet these requirements would be eligible for "conditional status," which would last for six years.

To move to the second phase of the citizenship process, undocumented immigrants would have to meet additional requirements, including the following:

- Attending college or serving in the U.S. military for at least two years
- Passing another criminal background check
- Demonstrating good moral character

Immigration rights activists show support for the DREAM Act during a 2010 rally in California. The bill has fueled debate about the rights of undocumented immigrants in the United States.

The DREAM Act would also allow undocumented immigrants to receive some types of federal financial aid for college. They would, for example, be eligible for work-study programs and student loans. But they could not receive federal grants, such as Pell grants.

The DREAM Act has won support from both Democrats and Republicans since it was first introduced in 2001. But the measure has repeatedly failed to clear both the House and Senate. In December 2010, the DREAM Act passed the House with a 216–198 vote. But ten days later, it failed to advance in the Senate by a 55–41 decision. The measure needed sixty votes to move forward.

Immigrants "Come Out" in Support of the DREAM Act

Over the years, the DREAM Act has fueled heated debate about the rights of undocumented immigrants in the United States. Those debates also triggered a nationwide movement among young undocumented immigrants. Many started to shed their cloaks of secrecy. They came out of the shadows to voice their support of the DREAM Act. These student activists—often called DREAMers—jeopardized their safety to publicly reveal they were undocumented immigrants. "The biggest obstacle we have is fear," DREAMer Viridiana Martinez told NPR. "So, coming out is a declaration that I am dropping the fear."

A Pulitzer Prize–winning journalist sent shock waves across the country in 2011 when he "came out" about his undocumented status. Reporter Jose Antonio Vargas, who emigrated from the Philippines when he was twelve years old, made the dangerous decision to reveal his status after Congress failed to pass the DREAM Act in 2010. The former *Washington Post* reporter said he was tired of living in fear and lying to people he respected. "I'm done running," he wrote in a story in the *New York Times*. "I'm exhausted. I don't want that life anymore."

The Debate Over the DREAM Act

The DREAM Act has won the support of immigration rights groups, military leaders, education officials, religious organizations, lawmakers on both sides of the aisle, and the Obama administration. President Obama repeated his support of the

Award-winning journalist Jose Antonio Vargas shocked the country in 2011 when he disclosed that he was an undocumented immigrant. The Philippines native said he was tired of living in fear.

DREAM Act during his 2012 State of the Union address. "Let's at least agree to stop expelling responsible young people who want to staff our labs, start new businesses, defend this country," the president said. "Send me a law that gives them the chance to earn their citizenship. I will sign it right away."

DREAM Act opponents argue the measure would increase the number of people who enter and stay in the country illegally. They also say the bill would grant amnesty—forgiveness of illegal acts—to undocumented immigrants.

The Federation for American Immigration Reform (FAIR) called the DREAM Act a "sweeping illegal alien amnesty bill" in 2009. The organization's president also said the DREAM Act would make it harder for American families to get jobs and send their children to college. "The DREAM Act would not only allow millions of newly legalized illegal aliens to compete for their jobs, but allow them to compete for their own children's educational opportunities," Dan Stein said in a March 2009 press release.

Representative Cliff Stearns of Florida echoed those concerns in 2010 when he voted against the DREAM Act. "We are a nation of laws and there is a right way to enter the country, and that is to wait your turn and to comply with our laws," he said in a December 2010 press release. In mid-2012, the DREAM Act remained in limbo.

A Major Policy Shift

Immigration rights activists, however, cheered President Obama's decision in June 2012 to stop deporting undocumented immigrants who came to the country as children. This major policy shift allowed undocumented immigrants who met specific criteria to work in the country legally. Under new rule, as many as 1.4 million unauthorized immigrants could escape the fear of deportation for two years—subject to renewal—and apply for authorization to work in the country.

The new policy applied to undocumented immigrants who came to the United States before they were sixteen years old; had lived continually in the country for five years; were in school, had graduated from high school, or had served in the military; had not been convicted of a serious crime; and were under the age of thirty.

President Obama called the policy change the "right thing to do" for the young undocumented immigrants who attended the same schools as U.S. children, pledged allegiance to the same flag, and were "Americans in their heart, in their minds, in every single way but one: on paper."

Critics called the president's new policy amnesty for undocumented immigrants. They also said it bypassed Congress and could make it more difficult to pass long-term immigration reform.

The president said the change would not grant amnesty to undocumented immigrants or resolve the divisive issues surrounding the country's immigration policies. He also said it wouldn't open a path to citizenship like the DREAM Act. The president's new policy wasn't etched in stone, either. It was an executive order that could be changed by future presidents.

Undocumented Immigrant Heroes

Many undocumented immigrants, however, have achieved their goals without the benefit of President Obama's new policy or the DREAM Act.

Dr. Alfredo Quinones-Hinojosa climbed a fence between Mexico and the United States when he was eighteen years old. He worked in hot, dusty fields and picked cotton, tomatoes, and cantaloupes, according to a story on NPR. He later went to Harvard Medical School and became a neurosurgeon. The Johns Hopkins University professor—and U.S. citizen—has done groundbreaking research in the treatment of brain cancer.

When he was thirteen, Dr. Harold Fernandez was smuggled into the United States on a "leaky boat crowded with illegal immigrants," according to a story in the New York Times. The Colombia

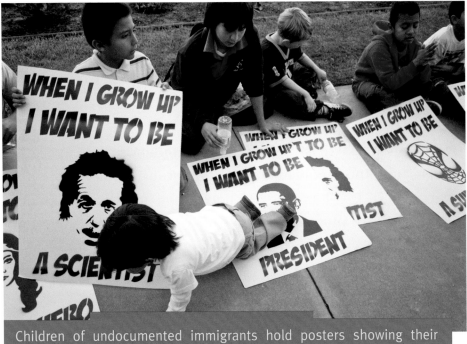

Children of undocumented immigrants hold posters showing their dreams for the future during a 2011 rally in Arizona. Many undocumented immigrants and their children are now successful professionals.

native became the valedictorian of his class at West New York's Memorial High School. He later went to Princeton University and Harvard Medical School. Dr. Fernandez is a U.S. citizen and a cardiac surgeon at St. Francis Hospital in Roslyn, New York.

Actor Carlo Alban kept a closely guarded secret about his immigration status when he starred in the children's television show *Sesame Street*. The teenager from Ecuador was an undocumented immigrant during the four years he worked on the popular show in the 1990s. "It was his dream job, but he was in constant fear of exposure," a story by the *BBC News Magazine* said. Alban and his family later became permanent U.S. residents. He continued to work in the entertainment industry and performed a one-man show based on his life.

Change Is Coming

Trail of Dreams activist Gaby Pacheco applauds these and other "heroes" in the undocumented immigrant community. What advice do DREAMers like Pacheco have for young, undocumented immigrants who hope they, too, can do something extraordinary with their lives?

- Remember that you are not alone.
- Ask for help from trusted teachers, counselors, church leaders, immigration rights activists, or volunteers at immigration centers in your communities.
- Find "sacred spaces" where your status isn't a burden. (Jose Ivan Arreola said his "sacred space" is the basketball court.)
- Never give up on your dreams.

"I believe in my heart that this situation is going to change and there will be a reform to our immigration system," Arreola said. "Not too long ago, people said African Americans didn't belong in white schools. Ideas change. And I believe it's only a matter of time before attitudes about undocumented immigrants change, too."

Glossary

activist A person who works for a specific cause or goal.

amnesty A general pardon for offenses against a government.

cocaine An addictive narcotic drug that comes from the leaves of coca plants.

deport To force a person who is not a citizen to leave a country.

detain To hold in custody.

discrimination The unfair treatment of people because of their race, gender, age, religion, or ethnic background.

empower To be given authority or a greater sense of confidence.

illegal alien A term sometimes used to describe a person who is in this country without legal documentation.

immigration The movement of nonnative people into a country in order to settle there.

impose To establish or apply by using authority.

Ku Klux Klan A hate group that believes in racial segregation and white supremacy.

odyssey A series of travels and adventures.

rhetoric Language that is intended to persuade or influence people.

suicide The act of intentionally taking one's own life.

undocumented Lacking documents required for legal immigration or residence.

visa An official document that allows someone to enter or leave a specific country.

Citizenship and Immigration Canada (CIC)

Ottawa, ON K1A 1L1

Canada

(888) 242-2100 (inside Canada)

Web site: http://www.cic.gc.ca

The CIC helps immigrants to Canada become citizens. It processes citizenship applications, requests for proof of citizenship, and searches of citizenship records.

Educators for Fair Consideration (E4FC)

2130 Fillmore Street, #248

San Francisco, CA 94115

Web site: http://www.e4fc.org

This advocacy group supports undocumented immigrants in their "pursuit of college, career, and contribution." Its Web site has many resources for undocumented students, including information about scholarships, financial aid, internships, and life after college.

Immigration Policy Center

American Immigration Council

1331 G Street NW, Suite 200

Washington, DC 20005-3141

(202) 507-7500

Web site: http://www.immigrationpolicy.org

This organization is the research and policy arm of the

American Immigration Council. Its Web site has a wealth of information about issues facing undocumented immigrants.

Pew Hispanic Center
1615 L Street NW, Suite 700
Washington, DC 20036
(202) 419-3600
Web site: http://www.pewhispanic.org
The Pew Hispanic Center is a research organization that "seeks to improve understandings" of the Hispanic population in this country. The center also studies issues facing undocumented immigrants in the United States.

U.S. Citizenship & Immigration Services
111 Massachusetts Avenue NW
Washington, DC 20529-2260
(800) 767-1833
Web site: http://www.uscis.gov
This federal agency oversees legal immigration into the United States. Its Web site has information and forms related to green cards and visas, working in the United States, and the citizenship process.

Web Sites

Due to the changing nature of Internet links, Rosen Publishing has developed an online list of Web sites related to the subject of this book. This site is updated regularly. Please use this link to access the list:

http://www.rosenlinks.com/FAQ/IMM

For Further Reading

Allport, Alan, and John E. Ferguson. *Immigration Policy* (Point-Counterpoint). 2nd ed. New York, NY: Chelsea House, 2009.

Alvarez, Julia. *Return to Sender*. New York, NY: Alfred A. Knopf, 2009.

Bausum, Ann. *Denied, Detained, Deported: Stories from the Dark Side of American Immigration*. Washington, DC: National Geographic, 2009.

Haugen, David M., and Susan Musser, eds. *Illegal Immigration* (Opposing Viewpoints). Farmington Hills, MI: Greenhaven Press, 2011.

Hina, Paul. *Illegal Immigration* (Contemporary Issues Companion). Farmington Hills, MI: Greenhaven Press, 2008.

Kleyn, Tatyana. *Immigration: The Ultimate Teen Guide* (It Happened to Me). Lanham, MD: Scarecrow Press, 2011.

Nazario, Sonia. *Enrique's Journey*. New York, NY: Random House, 2006.

Perl, Lila. *Immigration: This Land Is Whose Land?* (Controversy!) New York, NY: Marshall Cavendish Benchmark, 2010.

Restrepo, Bettina. *Illegal*. New York, NY: Katherine Tegen Books, 2011.

Streissguth, Thomas. *Welcome to America? A Pro/Con Debate Over Immigration*. (Issues In Focus Today). Berkeley Heights, NJ: Enslow, 2009.

Index

About the Author

Lisa Wade McCormick is an award-winning writer and investigative reporter. She has written fifteen nonfiction books for children and young adults. McCormick and her family live in Kansas City, Missouri. She often visits schools and libraries with her golden retriever, who is a Reading Education Assistance Dog (READ). The mission of the READ program is to improve children's literacy skills by giving struggling readers the opportunity to read to dogs.

Photo Credits

Cover © iStockphoto.com/Juan Estey; p. 5 © Elizabeth Flores/ Minneapolis Star Tribune/ZUMA Press; pp. 7, 8, 16, 18, 28, 33, 38, 41 © AP Images; p. 11 David McNew/Getty Images; pp. 13, 57 © Jack Kurtz/ZUMA Press; p. 21 Joshua Lott/Getty Images; p. 34 © Erik Lesser/ZUMA Press; pp. 44, 49, 54 The Washington Post/Getty Images; p. 52 Fresno Bee/MCT/Getty Images.

Designer: Evelyn Horowicz; Editor: Andrea Sclarow Paskoff; Photo Researcher: Amy Feinberg